A Decad

Ki

GW01454226

1960s

The Most Evil
Serial Killers of the
1960s

Jack Smith

Warning
Throughout the book, there are some descriptions of murders and crime scenes that some people might find disturbing. There might be also some language used by people involved in the murders that may not be appropriate.

Note
Words in italic are quoted words from verbatim and have been reproduced as is, including any grammatical errors and misspelled words.

ISBN: 9798615020605

MAPLEWOOD
— PUBLISHING —

www.maplewoodpublishing.com

Contents

A Brand-New Era

There can be no doubt that the 1960s were a turbulent time in America. It was a time of social and political transition in which standard bearers such as John F. Kennedy and Martin Luther King Jr. paid the price of leadership with their lives. And if these literal political hit jobs weren't bad enough, there were also plenty of psychotic killers lurking in the midst of the flower power gatherings in Haight-Ashbury and the like.

It was the 1960s, of course, that produced one of the most notorious criminals of all—Charles Mason. And although (as Manson readily told just about anyone who would listen to him) he had technically never been found to have personally killed anyone with his own hands, he was convicted of being the insidious orchestrator of one of the most infamous murder cults in history. Even before Mason, however, Charles Schmid, the so-called "Pied Piper of Tucson", was leading his own debauched teenaged minions on a rampage through civil society.

The 1960s was a time of radical thought that trickled down to just about every segment of the culture. There was a quiet revolution going on in the hearts and minds of men and women everywhere. Even the serial killers of this period often had their own warped agendas that they attempted to feed the masses in the midst of their atrocities. Cape Cod killer Tony Costa, for example, after being caught killing women in a drug-induced stupor, took every opportunity to trumpet his LSD-laced philosophies.

During this "Dawning of the Age of Aquarius", dope-smoking hippies hoped to usher in a brand-new age of enlightenment. But instead of ushering in an era of peace and love, the 1960s brought us the age of the serial killer. These are their stories.

William MacDonald
The Case of the
Walking Corpse

In June of 1924, a British baby boy named Allen
Ginsberg came into this world. He was followed in
June of 1926 by an American baby boy also
named Allen Ginsberg, and it would be most inapt
to confuse the two—one (the American) grew up
to be one of the finest poets of the Beat
Generation, while the other (the Brit) grew up to be
one of the worst serial killers of the 1960s.
Fortunately for clarity's sake, the British Ginsberg
changed his name to William MacDonald well
before becoming infamous as the Sydney
Mutilator, and it's MacDonald we'll call him from
this point forward.

So William MacDonald was born into a troubled
home in Liverpool, England. He had behavioral
problems early on, and as an adolescent, he was
diagnosed as a paranoid schizophrenic.
Nevertheless, when Britain's Darkest Hour came
at the outbreak of World War Two, the draft board
was in no position to be picky, and MacDonald
was drafted into the army along with the rest. He
had, as might be expected, a hard time adjusting.
He was routinely bullied, and one night in 1943 he
was even raped in an air-raid shelter by a member

of his own platoon. The rest of MacDonald's military service was similarly difficult, but he was not ultimately discharged until 1947.

His return to civilian life brought its own difficult adjustments, and once again MacDonald had a hard time making the transition. His brother recommended that he see a therapist—and after several sessions, the therapist decided that MacDonald was so crazy that he had him committed to an outright insane asylum. Stuffed in a small room with several other severely disturbed patients, MacDonald was forced to endure their incessant gibbering in between round after round of electroshock therapy. It was a horrific experience that only came to an end when his mother successfully petitioned for his release.

Shortly afterward, however, MacDonald complained of hearing voices and having hallucinations and was institutionalized again. Realizing that the treatments weren't helping him—were, in fact, making him worse—he decided that he would simply have to pretend to be normal. It worked, and he was soon discharged from the asylum. Perhaps to symbolize his changed attitude, he then legally changed his name from Allen Ginsberg to William MacDonald. And in 1949, he also changed his country, packing up his clothes and setting sail for Canada. Life in Canada proved unfulfilling for William MacDonald, however, and in 1955 he was off again, this time to Australia.

Meanwhile, MacDonald had finally come to grips with the fact that he was a homosexual. Of course, this was not something that was widely approved of back in the 1950s, and in Australia having relations with another man was in fact quite illegal. This meant that when MacDonald began to explore his urges, he had to do it in secret. Unfortunately, the public restroom he picked for his initial efforts wasn't quite secret enough, and one of the men he approached turned out to be an undercover detective. MacDonald was given two years of probation.

Realizing that he needed to take a different approach to express his sexuality, in 1961 MacDonald moved to Australia's capital of Sydney, rented a cheap apartment, and became a regular at the city's underground gay hangouts. And at one of these meeting places, MacDonald met Amos Hugh Hurst—the first man he would kill.

At 63, Amos was significantly older than MacDonald, but the two apparently hit it off. They both enjoyed drinking and soon became regular drinking buddies. During one of their sessions at a local bar, they decided to go back to Hurst's apartment together to drink some more. They continued until Hurst was so drunk that he was on the verge of blacking out. MacDonald didn't let his drinking buddy pass out peacefully, however. Placing his hands around Amos's neck, MacDonald squeezed until he began to vomit blood. Disgusted by his own handiwork, MacDonald then let go, reared back, and punched Amos as hard as he could, right in the face. Amos flew off the bed and fell in a crumpled heap on the floor. There he lay—and he would never get up again.

After MacDonald realized that Amos was dead, he took off his victim's pants and shoes, placed him in bed, and pulled the sheet over his head as if he were asleep. He then loitered around for a few moments, savoring his crime, before turning out the lights, locking up the apartment, and leaving. In the days after the murder, MacDonald eagerly awaited any news of the crime, sure he would soon hear that the police were looking for Amos Hurst's killer. Instead, a few days later he saw an obituary in the newspaper stating that Amos had died in his sleep! Either MacDonald had been extraordinarily successful at covering his tracks— or the cops who came upon Amos's body were negligent and lackadaisical in the extreme. At any rate, newly minted killer William MacDonald realized to his astonishment that he had quite literally just "gotten away with murder".

Thus emboldened to strike again, MacDonald found his next victim just sitting out on a park bench. It was midsummer in 1961 and 41-year-old Alfred Reginald Greenfield was simply enjoying the scenery when MacDonald approached him in a friendly enough manner, struck up a conversation, and eventually offered to buy him a drink. Instead of going to the local pub, though, MacDonald took Alfred to the local public baths, where those in Sydney's homosexual community were known to have secret liaisons. The two talked and drank as they sat by the side of a pool, and when Alfred eventually passed out drunk, MacDonald saw his moment.

Whipping out his knife, MacDonald savagely slashed open Alfred's neck. It was a rude awakening, and worse was to come; as Alfred gurgled his own blood, MacDonald repeatedly plunged the knife into his torso. Once Alfred succumbed, MacDonald took off the slain man's pants to perform one final outrage. Using the same bloody knife with which he had sliced open Alfred's neck, he meticulously sliced off his penis. He then gathered up Alfred's severed genitalia— along with his belongings—and fled the scene.

After this hideous incident, MacDonald lay low for a few months, but by autumn his desire to kill brought him out of the woodwork once again. On November 21st, MacDonald bought a vicious-looking knife with a 6-inch-long blade. That same evening he paid a visit to the local bath house, where he encountered a middle-aged man named Ernest Cobbin who was wobbling around and obviously inebriated. Sensing an easy target, MacDonald sat down next to Ernest and struck up a conversation. It wasn't long before he got the man alone and plied him with even more alcohol. While Ernest drank his final fill, the meticulous MacDonald surreptitiously donned a thin raincoat—then grabbed his knife and thrust it into Ernest's throat. As his blood splattered all over his raincoat-clad assailant, Ernest attempted to mount a defense, but he was unable to withstand MacDonald's repeated blows. Soon all the fight went out of him, and he slumped limp and lifeless in MacDonald's arms. Then, just as he had with Alfred Greenfield, MacDonald pulled Ernest's pants down and chopped off his penis.

When Ernest Cobbin's body was found the next day, the media worked itself into a complete frenzy. There seemed to be a twisted Jack the Ripper type killer on the loose in Sydney! People were equal parts angry and fearful—and they were also entirely bewildered. What kind of person goes around cutting off men's genitals? Fortunately, the police had a theory: perhaps the perpetrator was "jealous" of his victims! Unfortunately, they had no idea who the person suffering from the world's worst case of penis envy might be. With no name and no physical description, detectives were completely stumped (no macabre pun intended). So they simply dubbed the unknown assailant the "Mutilator", put a 10,000-dollar reward on his head, and hoped for the best.

Sadly, no leads turned up before MacDonald struck again in the spring of 1962. Meeting Frank Gladstone McLean on the street, MacDonald made no attempt to lure him to a private place and get him drunk. Instead, he attempted to dispatch Frank right out in the open. This proved to be ill-considered, and the assault was interrupted by the approach of a man and woman walking with their young child. MacDonald hastily extricated himself from the scene as the passersby, horrified at the sight of Frank McLean lying in a puddle of blood, ran off to call the police. The devious MacDonald, however, was still lurking in the nearby shadows, and as soon as he saw that the coast was clear, he sprinted back to finish Frank off. Before the couple came back with the cops, he even managed to find the time to pull his victim's pants down and cut off his penis, which he then put inside a Ziploc bag and took home as a grisly trophy.

Shortly after committing this atrocity, MacDonald left his job as a mail sorter at the local post office and opened his own deli—but not under his own name; he was now calling himself Alan Edward

Brenan. He also moved into a new apartment located just above the deli. Shortly thereafter, he came across one Patrick Joseph Hackett, a local homeless man who was regularly down on his luck—and who was a regular fixture at the local pubs. After becoming acquainted with Patrick at one such dive, MacDonald invited him back to his new apartment to drink some more. Accepting that invitation was the last poor decision Patrick would make in his unfortunate life.

As soon as they were behind closed doors, MacDonald, supposing that Patrick was already drunk enough not to pose a threat and not wanting to waste good liquor on a man who was about to be too dead to appreciate it, pulled out his knife and began stabbing him vigorously. Patrick fought back, however, and managed to make MacDonald stab his own hand during the course of the struggle. It was a very momentary moment of triumph, though, as an infuriated MacDonald then plunged the knife deep into Patrick's heart, which promptly stopped beating. MacDonald next attempted to conduct his signature move—sawing his victim's penis off of his mangled corpse—but half-drunk and bleeding badly from his hand, he couldn't do it before he passed out right there on the spot.

MacDonald woke up a few hours later to the gruesome aftermath of the horrific bloodbath. His hand was still bleeding and needed some serious medical attention, so he left Patrick's butchered body in his apartment and hied himself down to the emergency room of a nearby hospital. After getting stitched up, he went back home to deal with the mess he had made. First, he dragged the corpse downstairs and crammed it into the crawlspace underneath the deli. Then he began the tedious work of cleaning the blood-spattered walls and floors of his apartment. It was no use, however; the blood had soaked into (and in some places clean through) the floorboards and could not be removed.

With no hope of tidying up, MacDonald decided to simply ditch his digs and run off. Breaking his lease and fleeing the scene, he made his way to the city of Brisbane and took up residence at a cheap boarding house. Fearful that the police would be hot on his trail, he grew some facial hair and plastered his head with dark hair-dye. It wasn't the most ingenious of disguises, but he figured it was better than nothing. Besides, if simply pulling a sheet over the body of Amos Hurst had worked so well, why shouldn't this?

As it turned out, MacDonald's attempt at disguise was beside the point. As the days passed, he didn't see a single word in the news about the death of his latest victim. It seems that none of the neighbors noticed anything amiss at his former place of business for quite some time. When the police finally did come to investigate, Patrick Hackett's remains were so deteriorated that they couldn't determine exactly how he had died. In fact, they couldn't even determine exactly who he was, and so—while it may sound like gross negligence by today's standards—they simply assumed that the body belonged to the building's registered tenant, Alan Edward Brennan—AKA William MacDonald! With no evidence of foul play, they shrugged, recorded the death as due to natural causes, and closed the case.

MacDonald had gotten off the hook once again. Not only that, everyone who knew him as Alan Brennan thought that he was dead. He was free and clear—until he went back to Sydney and was spotted on the street by a former coworker, John McCarthy. The startled man ran up to him and exclaimed, "I believed you had died!"

Annoyed, MacDonald merely grunted, "Leave me alone!" Then he simply sauntered off and, realizing that returning to Sydney hadn't been the best idea he'd ever had, kept sauntering all the way to Melbourne.

John McCarthy, meanwhile, went to the police to notify them that the reports of Alan Edward Brennan's death were greatly exaggerated. The cops didn't want to hear it, however, and just told

John to go home and sober up—and if that didn't work, to find himself a good psychiatrist! Not so easily rebuffed, John then took his story straight to the papers. He found a more receptive audience at the *Daily Mirror*, which published his account in an article headlined "The Case of the Walking Corpse".

Thus publicly prompted, the police reluctantly reopened the case, reopened "Brennan's" grave, and fingerprinted the corpse. The prints were clearly those of Patrick Joseph Hackett rather than Alan Edward Brennan. The police, badly embarrassed at having failed to take this simple step in the first place, rushed to make amends. They circulated a composite drawing of MacDonald to all of Australia's major newspapers, and he was quickly recognized and arrested in Melbourne.

Upon being taken into custody, MacDonald readily admitted his guilt. He was given five consecutive life sentences and stashed away in a maximum security psych ward, where he lived to the ripe old age of 90, finally passing away on May 12, 2015.

It All Depends on the Zodiac

The case of the Zodiac Killer, who left a string of innocents dead in late-60s California, is one of the most chilling serial killer cases of all time—mostly because some fifty years after the fact, it still remains unsolved! The Zodiac's MO was to kill and then taunt the papers and the public with cryptic letters to the editor. He would ultimately boast of killing 37 different people, although the official count of victims tallied by police stands at only seven.

The first two were 17-year-old David Arthur Faraday and his 16-year-old girlfriend Betty Lou Jensen, gunned down by the Zodiac on December 20, 1968. The next were Michael Renault Mageau and his girlfriend Darlene Elizabeth Ferrin, who were shot in a parking lot on the Fourth of July, 1969. Michael survived the shooting, but Darlene perished.

Next on the Zodiac's hit list were Bryan Calvin Hartnell and Cecelia Ann Shepard, whom he stabbed as they hung out by Lake Berryessa in Napa County on September 27, 1969. The couple was picnicking on a small peninsula jutting out into the lake when they were rudely interrupted by a "white man, about 5 feet 11 inches, weighing more than 170 pounds, with combed greasy brown hair" who ran up to them waving a gun. Wearing clip-on sunglasses over his eyes and a hood over his head, the stranger had a startling appearance— and an even more startling story.

He told the terrified youths that he had just escaped from prison and needed their car and all of their money so that he could make a break for it. He instructed Cecelia to tie up her boyfriend, then tied her up himself. It seemed that they were about to be the victims of a robbery. But then, for no explicable reason, the madman pulled out a knife and began stabbing his hogtied hostages. Bryan was stabbed six times, Cecilia a total of ten. As they lay bleeding, they saw their attacker sprinting back through the wilderness.

He was headed for Bryan's car, but not to steal it. Instead, he used a black felt-tip pen to scrawl the cryptic message *Vallejo/12-20-68/7-4-69/Sept 27-69-6:30/by knife*. Later that evening, he called up the local police station from a payphone and stated that he wanted to "report a murder". Shortly into the call, however, he revised his story to reveal that he himself was the murderer. And on this insane note, the Zodiac abruptly hung up.

The cops quickly traced the call to a payphone near a car wash just down the street from the police station. Racing over, they found the phone dangling off the hook as if the caller had just fled the scene. Detectives were able to lift a palm print from the phone but unable to match it to anything.

The victims, meanwhile, were discovered by a local fisherman when he heard their bloodcurdling screams. Although Bryan would survive his injuries, Cecelia passed away a couple of days later on September 29th.

The last confirmed Zodiac killing was that of Paul Lee Stine, who was shot dead in San Francisco on October 11th. Paul was a taxi driver, and the Zodiac Killer had apparently been his passenger to the intersection of Washington and Maple Streets. Once the cab came to a stop, however, the Zodiac pulled out his gun and shot Paul in the head. The aftermath of this murder was witnessed by a group of teenagers, who saw the killer take the dead driver's wallet and car keys before stepping out of the cab, wiping it down, and then simply strolling away from the scene. The teenagers knew better than to try to stop the madman themselves, but by the time they got the police on the scene, he was long gone. (One Officer Fouke later reported that he had actually seen the suspect on a nearby street but failed to stop him because he had been given an inaccurate description.)

Initially, the police believed that Paul had been killed in an ordinary robbery, but on October 13th the Zodiac Killer sent a letter to the papers claiming responsibility. His face—or a reasonable facsimile thereof—also made the papers, as the teenage witnesses helped a police artist produce a composite sketch of the murderer. In this picture, we see a man with a mild-mannered yet somehow sinister countenance. There is nothing at all remarkable about the drab and dour face peering up from the paper; the man looks as if he could be someone's dentist or accountant. In other words, this serial killer could have been anyone, and this kept the sketch from being of much use in identifying him.

Whoever he was, though, he seemed to be worried—not that he was going to get caught, but that he wasn't going to get proper credit for his crimes! Because on October 14th, the papers received another message from the Zodiac, and this one came with a startling artifact—a bloodied piece of a T-shirt. The taunting letter that accompanied it explained that it was a piece of Paul Stine's shirt that had been ripped from his corpse and that the writer was using it as confirmation that he was indeed the killer.

These letters to the editor were the most haunting thing about this case by far, the factor that made it nationally famous. The killer had sent his first missive to the *Vallejo Times Herald, San Francisco Examiner*, and *San Francisco*

Chronicle, apparently to introduce himself to the public and claim ownership of his killings: *I like killing people because it is so much fun. It is more fun than killing wild game in the forest because man is the most dangerous animal of all to kill. Something [when killing] gives me the most thrilling experience—it is even better than getting your rocks off with a girl. The best part of it is that when I die I will be reborn in paradise and the [people] I have killed will become my slaves for my afterlife.*

It was in another letter, sent to the *San Francisco Examiner* on August 7, 1969, that the killer first identified himself as the Zodiac. He was straight to the point: "Dear Editor, this is the Zodiac speaking." Although that was clear enough, the Zodiac's letters, in general, were so full of bad grammar and punctuation mistakes that it was often hard for investigators to make heads or tails of them. Yet he was a prolific writer, and he would continue to taunt the community with his communications for the next several years, until the very last known Zodiac letter emerged in January of 1974.

Among other things, this bizarre, rambling letter praised the recently released movie *The Exorcist*. It ended by stating, "ME = 37, SFPD = 0". In this "final score", the Zodiac was apparently taunting the San Francisco Police Department (SFPD) by saying that his final kill count came to 37 (a figure that has never been proven) while the police had scored a zero for their efforts. This was the last macabre jibe that the miscreant ever sent out, and after that, not another word was heard.

No one knows for sure what happened to this monster. Did he simply go back to living a normal life after wrecking the lives of so many others? Could he even now be a retired old man somewhere, living on social security? Or perhaps he perished long ago and took his secret with him to the grave? No one knows for sure, but this case is one that continues to haunt the residents of San Francisco to this very day.

Albert DeSalvo
The Measuring Man

Albert DeSalvo had a difficult upbringing to say the least. His father was a violent drunk who openly cheated on his wife, sometimes bringing his mistresses home to have liaisons with them right under her nose. He beat her, too, and on occasion, he beat DeSalvo simply because he "didn't move fast enough" when ordered to go fetch something.

Victimized by his father, it wasn't long before DeSalvo began to find victims of his own. Like many serial killers, before he ever harmed human beings, he took his aggression out on the animal kingdom. One of his favorite childhood pastimes was putting a cat and a dog together in a small crate so he could watch them maul each other to death. As he got holder, he graduated to petty crimes such as breaking into homes in his neighborhood.

At 17, though, DeSalvo seemingly tried to turn his life around by enlisting in the military. Sent to the Cold War hotspot of Berlin, he soon wed a young German woman whom he brought back to America when his overseas tour ended. In 1955 he was stationed at Fort Dix in New Jersey, and it was here that his antisocial habits began to resurface with abandon. DeSalvo began to act out in many ways, but by far the worst of his misbehavior occurred when he forced himself on a 9-year-old girl. The only reason he wasn't locked up for his horrendous offense was because he somehow convinced the child's mother to not go to the police.

DeSalvo's wife, meanwhile, was getting fed up with his "excessive sex drive"—as well as the back-to-back pregnancies that resulted therefrom. And as the mouths he had to feed multiplied, DeSalvo found himself needing not just more sex but more money. To supplement his income, he took to burglary, and to case the houses he planned to rob, he came up with a routine that simultaneously satisfied his sexual perversity. Pretending to be a talent scout from a local modeling agency, he would talk his way into the homes of local housewives. These visits would inevitably become creepy when DeSalvo whipped out a measuring tape and insisted on getting his hostess's measurements. Fortunately for these women, at this point, he wasn't doing anything more untoward than ogling their figures. But his leering eyes as he took their measurements were frightening enough that several of them reported the intrusive fraudster to police, earning DeSalvo his first nom de crime: the Measuring Man.

Shortly afterward, DeSalvo was arrested for attempting to break into a home. It was the spring of 1961, and DeSalvo was 30 years old. If the judge had given him a stiff sentence, this could have been a major turning point for him, but after serving a measly two years, DeSalvo hit the streets and picked up exactly where he let off.

Well, not exactly—this time around, he did a whole lot worse than just taking women's measurements and burglarizing their houses. Donning the uniform of a repairman/technician, he began to show up at homes around Massachusetts. He would gain the trust of women who were home alone and convince them that he needed to come inside to work on some utility or household appliances. He would then sexually assault them. It is said that he preyed upon literally hundreds of women in this fashion over the next two years. In Boston, however, matters were even worse, because some eleven women were not only raped but also strangled to death. These cases gave DeSalvo his next, and most famous, nickname: the Boston Strangler.

In 1964, DeSalvo was identified by one of his surviving victims and arrested. He quickly confessed and was placed in a psych ward at Bridgewater State Hospital. Although he claimed to be the Boston Strangler, he worked out a plea deal that had him prosecuted only for the serial rapes. This alone, however, was enough to give him a life sentence—but it turned out to be a short one, as DeSalvo was murdered by another prisoner in 1973, at 42 years of age.

Since then, some doubt has been cast as to whether DeSalvo was the Boston Strangler at all. Some suspect that DeSalvo made the whole thing up just to get attention, and others contend that the police, anxious to close a notorious case, pressured him into pretending that he was the killer. In 2001, the body of one of the Strangler's last victims, Mary Sullivan, was exhumed in order to gather new NDA evidence. The DNA that was gleaned did not match Albert DeSalvo. This does not necessarily mean he was innocent, but it does indeed make one wonder. Were the Measuring Man and the Boston Strangler one and the same? And if it wasn't DeSalvo who killed all of those women—then who was it?

The Brutality of Brudos
The Serial Killer with a
Foot Fetish

Even for a serial killer, Jerry Brudos was a strange man. And his strangest predilection was for feet. Since he was a small child, Brudos was obsessed with feet—but most especially, he was obsessed with female feet. When he was about five years old, he was out dumpster diving at a local junkyard when he came across a set of ladies' boots that he liked. He liked them so much, in fact, that he took them home to try them on. When his mother came home to find him traipsing around the house in the female footwear, she took the boots away and gave him a good spanking. This did not do much to deter him, however—the following year he got in trouble at school for stealing his teacher's shoes!

By the time he was a teenager, Brudos was regularly sneaking into neighbors' homes to take whatever female footwear he could find. Soon he was also stealing panties and lingerie. Obviously, no good was going to come of the path he was on, but he continued blithely on down it. By the time he was 16 he was actively harassing women, and this culminated him pulling a knife on a classmate and ordering her to take her clothes off. The girl fled instead, and young Jerry Brudos took a long overdue trip to the police station.

Deemed—with good reason—to be mentally unbalanced, he was thence sent to a mental hospital for monitoring. Here he opened up to staff doctors about all of his horrible fantasies, many of which focused on raping and torturing women. You would think that this might have given the counselors a bit of pause, but apparently, the facility was so overcrowded that even someone as admittedly threatening as Brudos couldn't be kept locked up indefinitely. As a result, he was discharged less than a year later, just in time to graduate from high school on schedule.

Brudos then enlisted in the military, but even the military couldn't handle his strange behavior, and he was quickly discharged. Next, trying his luck as an electrician, he learned the ropes quickly and was soon doing fairly well for himself. He also met a teenaged girl named Darcie, got her pregnant, and then married her. Darcie came from a troubled home, and although Brudos wasn't exactly a knight in shining armor, he appeared to be a means of escape for her. But she soon became weary of his seemingly insatiable sexual appetite—and most especially his penchant for wearing her underwear, something she caught him doing on more than a few occasions.

Brudos's real crime spree began in 1968 when he killed a door-to-door encyclopedia saleswoman named Linda Slawson. Brudos feigned interest in buying a set of encyclopedias and invited Linda into his home. He then lured her into the basement, got the drop on her, and smashed her in the face with a wooden board. He kept right on smashing until he was sure she was dead, then went right for the part of the female anatomy he liked best—the feet. He hacked the left one clean off, and while he would eventually discard the remainder of Linda's remains, this foot he kept as his morbid prized possession. As sickening as it sounds, he stored the foot in his freezer and would periodically take it out to dress it up in high heeled shoes.

At the tail end of 1968 Brudos found his next victim, a young woman named Jan Whitney. He lured her into his vehicle and strangled her with a leather strap, and then, like a twisted serial killing spider hauling a fly back to his insidious web, he hauled her body into his garage. After having intercourse with her mortal remains, he sliced off one of her breasts as a souvenir before dumping her corpse into a nearby river.

A few months after this horrid act, Brudos found a new victim in the form of Karen Sprinkler. He killed her in the same garage shop of horrors, sexually assaulted her corpse in the same manner, and then one-upped himself by slicing off *both* of her breasts before getting rid of her body.

Just a few weeks later, the killer struck again, this time tricking a young woman named Linda Salee into getting in his car by pretending to be a police officer. Seeing his fake badge, she obediently stepped inside—only to be hauled away to that same dastardly garage, where she was strangled to death. But death didn't end the horrors to which this poor woman was subjected. Like some mad serial killer scientists, Brudos attempted to create his own version of Frankenstein's monster. He hung Linda's body from the ceiling and then stuck her with hypodermic needles connected to electric wires. Putting his experience as an electrician to work in the worst way imaginable, he then sent a massive current straight to the dead woman's heart to see if he could bring her back to life—or at least get her nervous system to react and make her jump and dance around like a macabre marionette. Even for a serial killer, this man was clearly about as diabolically depraved as they come!

Fortunately for other women in the area, though, this was about the end of Brudos's slaughter spree. The police had begun to collect the bodies of his victims, and after information came in about a man matching his description harassing young women, they put two and two together and arrived at his residence with a search warrant. Just one look at his garage and they knew they had their man.

Jerry Brudos was put on trial in the summer of 1968, found guilty, and handed multiple life sentences, ensuring that this fiend would never see the light of day ever again. He died in prison on March 28, 2006.

The Kooky Case of
Edgar Cooke

Eric Edgar Cooke came from a working class background in Australia, where toil and dedication were more important than anything else. Even so, he seemed to have been born with a losing hand. Deformed with a harelip as a child, he was routinely mocked and ridiculed by his peers. His life at home wasn't much better since his booze-hound father was always eager to beat him within an inch of his life. Cooke responded by internalizing all of his anger and hatred, maintaining a mild-mannered exterior while a murderous rage was simmering just under the surface.

This rage first emerged when he was 18 years old and was booked on several counts of arson and burglary. Despite the seriousness of these crimes, the judge, no doubt considering his youth, decided to go easy on him and sentenced him to just three years in prison. When he got out, he managed to get steady work as a truck driver, wed a local woman, moved to the suburbs, and even became a full-fledged member of the neighborhood church. Despite his troubled past, Cooke now had all of the trappings of a normal life.

This, though, was nothing but a facade. He continued to break the law through petty thefts, breaking and entering, and peeping into women's windows at night. These aberrations, however, were nothing compared to the sick fantasies that were rolling around in his mind.

Although it can't be known for sure, Cooke's earliest murder is believed to have occurred in 1959. The victim, a 22-year-old woman who lived by herself, was sound asleep when an intruder snuck into her home. She woke up to a real-life nightmare, with someone standing over her and stabbing her multiple times.

If Cooke truly was the culprit, then he must have laid low a while, because his next murder didn't occur until January 27, 1963. And it must be noted that this killing was a lot different from the 1959 crime. Instead of sneaking into a home and stabbing someone unawares, Cooke embarked on a random shooting spree. Stumbling on a parked car with a couple inside, he began firing rapidly into the vehicle. The couple, although injured, survived the fusillade, but others were not so lucky that night. A couple of teenaged boys were shot dead on the street, and then the self-appointed arbiter of death walked up to a nearby house, knocked on the door, and shot the man who answered it point blank in the face.

Cooke struck again on February 16th when he burglarized an apartment. Waking the sleeping 24-year-old resident, he proceeded to strangle her with the cord from the lamp on her nightstand. He then took his time violating her corpse before ditching it outside, arranged in a vulgar position. The young lady's terrified neighbors discovered this bizarre and wretched scene the following day.

A few months later, Cooke returned to random gunfire as his MO, shooting an unsuspecting 18-year-old babysitter in the head. His days were numbered, however, and his crime spree was coming to an end. Cooke had been storing his assault rifle in some bushes, and one fine day in 1963, a pair of retirees just happened to stumble upon the weapon poking out of the shrubbery. They notified the police, who immediately suspected that the weapon had been left by the perpetrator of the recent shootings, which had occurred quite close to where the rifle was found.

Wisely deciding to let the rifle remain where it was, the police placed several undercover officers in the area to watch and wait for the owner to come back. It took a couple of weeks, but Cooke did indeed return, and the police immediately apprehended him. He was tried that very November, found guilty as charged, sentenced to death, and hanged just over a year later.

Wayne Boden's Wicked World

Like so many others who have committed this caliber of crime, Wayne Boden seemed to be in a wicked world all his own. How did this man become so twisted? He actually began life with a fair amount of promise. He was well liked in his Canadian high school, and he even played on the football team. Shortly after he graduated, however, his life began to go downhill—and by the fall of 1968, the 20-year-old Boden was actively plotting his first murder.

His first victim was a mild-mannered young teacher named Norma Vailancourt who lived in a busy section of downtown Montreal, Quebec. Montreal was even then a vibrant capital and a dynamic crossroads of culture, a big city to be sure, but one thing that separated it from its urban counterparts was its fairly low crime rate. Gruesome murders just weren't very common at all. So when this unassuming schoolmarm was found choked to death in her apartment, sexually assaulted and with savage bite marks all over her breasts, the community was alarmed, to say the least.

Still, after a whole year passed without one further sign of the dastardly killer, tensions were starting to ease. Then, on October 3, 1969, Boden struck again. His new victim, Shirley Audette, was strangled, raped, and bitten on her breasts just like Norma Vailancourt. The circumstances were so similar that even a casual observer could have told you that the killings were connected, and it wasn't long before the police realized that they had a true-blue serial killer on their hands.

Not only that, the killer soon proved that he was picking up the pace. In November of 1969, 20-year-old Marielle Archambault was found dead in the same exact horrid state as the previous two victims. Marielle had been working at a jewelry store, and when she didn't come into work as scheduled, her coworkers became concerned. Her boss actually went over to her apartment building, and after voicing her concerns to Marielle's landlady, she was able to gain access to her apartment. They found Marielle's fully clothed corpse propped up on the couch as if purposefully posed. Her clothes were on, concealing the trauma she had sustained, but underneath them, police discovered clear signs of sexual assault—along with several puncture wounds to her breasts. These bite marks led the local papers to dub this increasingly prolific serial killer the Vampire Rapist.

It wasn't long before this vampire struck again, sexually assaulting and killing Jean Way. Jean's body was discovered by her boyfriend, Brian Caulfield. The two had planned on spending the evening together, and so when Brian showed up and knocked on her door, he naturally expected her to answer. When she didn't, he eventually gave up and left, but he returned about an hour later to see if she had come home. She still didn't answer the door, but when he tried the knob he found that it was unlocked. Growing more concerned by the second, Brian went ahead and stepped inside. Seeing the apartment in disarray, he made his way to Marielle's bedroom, where he saw something he would never forget. There was his girlfriend, stripped naked and sprawled out on her bed cold and lifeless.

It would later be determined that Marielle was most likely still alive when Brian first knocked on her door. Even more disturbing, Boden was apparently in the middle of his assault when Brian arrived on the scene. But since this dastardly killer had been prudent enough to lock the door behind him, Brian was completely unaware that the love of his life was being mercilessly defiled and murdered even while he was standing right there on the other side of the door.

By New Year's, the police were already closing in, and Boden, feeling the pressure, ditched Montreal for the city of Calgary some 2,200 miles away in Western Canada. Here he would hunt down his final victim, Elizabeth Porteous. Police who converged on the scene of her murder received a valuable tip from her friends that she had recently been seeing a man named Bill who drove a blue Mercedes. Calgary cops were instructed to keep an eye out for the car, and sure enough, the next day it was spotted just down the street from Elizabeth's residence. Undercover officers hid nearby and waited for the owner to appear. As soon as they saw him, they pounced and placed him under arrest without incident.

The man they apprehended was Wayne Clifford Boden. Further linking him to the killings was the fact that one of Boden's cufflinks had been found at one of the crime scenes. When questioned, however, Boden stated that while he knew the victim, he hadn't killed her. He claimed that she had been alive when he left her and that he had no idea what had happened to her after that. Despite his denials, however, the forensic team had an ace up their sleeve. The bite marks on all of the victims' breasts had been closely examined and documented, and when compared to Boden's dental records, they were found to be an exact match. This case made history as the very first time in Canada that someone was found guilty of murder based on this kind of dental forensic evidence.

Boden was given multiple life sentences, without the remotest possibility of parole. Nevertheless, he still managed to find his way outside of prison walls one more time—in fact, he managed to escape. The incident occurred in 1977 when he was granted some time out on a day pass. He ate lunch at a nearby restaurant under the strict supervision of a couple of guards and a social worker. But his minders apparently got just a little bit too comfortable with the congenial Boden, and after they let him go unescorted to the bathroom, he disappeared. As it turns out, Boden managed to climb out a bathroom window and hop down to the street.

Making matters even more absurd, just days before his breakout Boden had somehow talked a sales rep at American Express into giving him a credit card! It remains unclear how Amex expected a convict who made 99 cents a month working on prison projects to pay his credit card bill, but Boden was given a card all the same. After his escape, he used it to buy food and beer at a local bar. His good times came to a quick end, though, when his guards caught up with him and hauled him back to prison.

That was about the worst thing that they could do to Boden, but of course, his negligent guards and the social worker received severe reprimands, and American Express had to conduct an internal investigation to figure out how a credit card was issued to an infamous inmate serving a life sentence. After this last gasp of freedom, Boden remained in prison until March 27, 2006, when he passed away from cancer.

Ian Brady and Myra Hindley
The Moors Murders

One serial killer is bad enough, two serial killers are worse—and a serial killer couple working as a team is about as bad as it gets. In fact, Ian Brady and Myra Hindley were responsible for one of the worst serial murder sprees in British history, known as the Moors murders.

Brady was definitely the predominant force between the two. Like many psychopaths, he had been a vulnerable child raised under uncertain conditions. Abandoned by his biological parents, he had grown up in foster homes in a rough section of the rough Scottish city of Glasgow. Falling in with the wrong crowd was customary around there, and soon Brady was getting regularly arrested for petty crimes. In order to get him away from the bad influences around him, he was eventually transferred to Manchester, England. But the move failed to straighten him out; his disciplinary problems continued, and by the time he was 18 he was relegated to a youth facility.

It was after his discharge that he met a young woman named Myra Hindley. Hindley hailed from a Manchester suburb called Gorton, and she was for all intents and purposes a good kid—she was even a regular churchgoer. Hindley's life took a decided turn when she met Ian Brady, however. Fascinated by what she viewed as his "dark and cunning genius", Hindley readily discarded her old values as she became an avid disciple of Brady's warped and twisted philosophies. She was also more than willing to fulfill his fantasies. Brady apparently had a thing for Nazis, and he convinced Hindley to dress up as one—as well as undress while he snapped photos of their deviance.

But even Hindley's enthusiastic compliance with his deviant demands wasn't enough for Brady. Soon, he felt he needed to make some of his darker fantasies a reality. So one day he sat Myra down and informed her that he intended to carry out "the perfect murder". This wasn't the first time that Brady had made such macabre and grandiose plans, and Hindley probably didn't know whether he was serious or not. Nevertheless, she agreed to go along with him, and the two began planning how they would make their first kill. They agreed that Hindley would drive a van while Brady drove behind her on his motorcycle looking for potential targets. Brady would then flash his headlight when he found one.

The first he spotted was an 8-year-old girl who was playing outside, but Hindley, whether out of last-minute compassion or pragmatic fear, vetoed this choice and kept right on driving no matter how much the frustrated Brady flashed his headlight. She would later claim that the reason she refused to target the youngster was that she was a "neighbor of her mother's".

The next girl they encountered was not so lucky—even though 16-year-old Pauline Reade was actually a classmate of Hindley's own sister Maureen. Pauline was walking to a dance when Brady saw her. He signaled Hindley, and this time she obligingly pulled over and struck up a conversation with Pauline. She managed to lure the girl into her van, claiming she needed help to find an expensive glove she had lost. Shortly thereafter, Brady came up and joined the search. Hindley told Pauline to go with him and look for the glove while she stayed in the van, and with seemingly nothing to fear, she readily agreed. Her trust would be horribly betrayed.

About half an hour later, Brady returned alone. He then took Hindley back to where Pauline Reade was breathing her last, mortally wounded by severe cuts to her throat that had almost taken her head clean off. Hindley could also see that her clothing was disheveled and that she showed signs of having been sexually assaulted. Hindley asked Brady if he had raped Pauline, to which Brady—as if it were a no-brainer—responded, "Of course I did!" When Pauline succumbed, Brady buried her body and the two drove off as if nothing had happened.

The next person the couple targeted was a 12-year-old kid named John Kilbride, whom they came across at a local market on November 23, 1963. They offered to give him a ride home, and he hopped inside Hindley's van. It wasn't long before they made a detour to the moor, offering as their rationale the same lame story they had given Pauline: that they were making a pit stop to look for a glove that Hindley had lost on the moor. And just like before, Hindley waited in the car while Brady took the boy with him under the pretense of looking for the glove. Once they reached a remote location, Brady turned on the child, brutally assaulting him before slitting his throat and ultimately choking him to death with a pair of shoelaces.

The duo wouldn't strike again until the following summer, when on June 16, 1964, they intercepted another 12-year-old boy, Keith Bennett, who was headed to his grandma's house. The two solicited the trusting child's help to load boxes into Hindley's van. Instead, of course, they drove Keith to their murderous stomping ground on the moor. Once again they used the lost glove ploy, and after Keith went out with Brady to look for it, Brady once again sexually assaulted his victim before choking him to death.

The day after Christmas, the maniacs were at it again, accosting a 10-year-old girl named Lesley Ann Downey. Their modus operandi started out the same as last time as they asked Lesley's help in loading items into their van, but rather than take her to the moor, they convinced her to go home with them. There they ripped off her clothes and forced her to pose for nude photos. After that, they sexually assaulted her and choked her to death with Brady's weapon of choice—a shoestring. The next day, they drove her dead body to the moor and buried it along with all of the other victims.

The pair's final victim was also the oldest. At 17, apprentice engineer Edward Evans was just a few years younger than his killers. Brady befriended Edward and pretended that Hindley was his sister rather than his girlfriend—this in order to lure the young man in by making him think that Hindley might be a potential love interest. Inviting Edward back to Hindley's house, they proceeded to drink and hang out with each other. As the evening wore on, Brady had the idea of inviting Hindley's brother-in-law, David Smith, over to the party. David was married to Hindley's little sister Maureen, and Brady was on pretty good terms with him—the two liked each other, and Brady apparently believed that he could bring David into his and Hindley's twisted inner circle. It was his intention to initiate David into their wicked little world that very night.

But it turned out that David wasn't quite prepared for what he was about to witness. As he would later tell police when he first arrived, he was ushered into the kitchen while Brady said he was going to the living room to get some wine: *I waited about a minute or two, then suddenly I heard a hell of a scream; it sounded like a woman, really high pitched. Then the screams carried on, one after another, really loud. Then I heard Myra shout, "Dave, help him!" When I ran in, I just stood inside the living room and I saw a young lad. He was lying with his head and shoulders on the couch and his legs were on the floor. He was facing upwards. Brady was standing over him, facing him, with his legs on either side of the young lad's legs. The lad was still screaming. Brady had a hatchet in his hand. He was holding it above his head and he hit the lad on the left side of his head with the hatchet. I heard the blow, it was a terrible hard blow, it sounded horrible.* Brady then strangled Edward with an electrical cord, after which the wretched group stashed his body in a spare bedroom and made plans to take it to the moor the next day and bury it with all the rest.

David, though, didn't have the stomach to follow through with the plan. Shortly after he returned home to his waiting wife Maureen, he broke down and told her everything that had transpired. Shocked and horrified, Maureen advised him to call the police. Never mind the fact that her own sister was involved; she was adamant that these killers needed to be turned into the authorities before they struck again.

So that's what David did. First thing in the morning, he phoned up the police, who promptly came over and drove him down to the police station. He told them everything he had seen and everything else he knew about Brady and Hindley, and shortly afterward Brady was arrested on suspicion of murder. When his trial convened on April 16, 1966, David Smith served as the primary witness for the prosecution.

Initially, it seemed certain that both Brady and Hindley would receive the death penalty, but as the UK abolished capital punishment while they were on trial, they were both given life in prison instead. They eventually died there, Myra Hindley in 2002 and Ian Brady in 2017.

Lucian Staniak
Poland's Maniac

When it comes to crime, Poland may not break into the world news as much as some other nations, but back in the 1960s, the country was in the grip of one of the worst spates of serial murder in its history.

Like the Zodiac Killer, Lucian Staniak was fond of sending letters to the editor about his evil exploits. In fact, he sent his first one even before he committed his first murder, proclaiming to one of Warsaw's main newspapers that "There is no happiness without tears, no life without death. Beware: I am going to make you cry!" Instead of crying, the editors in that newsroom most likely had a good laugh as they shook their heads about their crazed correspondent—but when the disemboweled corpse of a young woman was discovered in a public park in the nearby town of Olsztyn the next day, it suddenly didn't seem so funny. Neither did the follow-up message that declared, "I picked a juicy flower in Olsztyn and I shall do it again somewhere else, for there is no holiday without a funeral."

There was obviously a true psychopathic killer on the loose, but as everyone stood on edge wondering what would happen next... nothing

49

happened at all. Indeed, it would be six full months before Lucian Staniak struck again. Folks in Poland had just rung in the New Year when in January of 1965 the mutilated corpse of a teenage girl turned up in a factory basement. She had been abducted on her way home from school, sexually assaulted, sliced open, and then abandoned.

Staniak then once again laid low for a while, waiting until November before striking again. His victim was another young girl, whom he accosted at a train station. He apparently knocked her out with chloroform before raping her, and after he was finished with that he continued his brutality by repeatedly sticking a screwdriver into her vagina. Even after she was dead, Staniak continued his cruelty, placing her corpse inside a packing crate and jamming a metal spike into her vagina. The very next day he fired off another missive to the newspaper in which he voiced his sadistic, poetastrical musings: "Only tears of sorrow can wash out the stain of shame; only pangs of suffering can blot out the fires of lust."

Following his now established pattern, Staniak again dropped out of sight, only to reemerge six months later in early May of 1966 to target yet another teenage girl. This time he left her brutalized corpse right out in the open, apparently taunting authorities with his brazenness. The police were indeed immensely frustrated at their inability to get a lead in the case, and they would have to wait another six months for their breakthrough.

In December of 1966, 17-year-old Janina Kozielska was found brutalized in horrific fashion at the train station. Her killer had left a chilling note: "I have done it again."

What followed was just good old-fashioned detective work. The police quickly discovered that Janina's littler sister had been one of the killer's previous victims. This led them to conclude that he was an acquaintance of some kind. Well, where did the sisters know him from? A little bit of further probing revealed that both of them had done some modeling at the Krakow Art Lover's Club. This then reminded detectives that all of the killer's letters to the editor had been scrawled in red paint. Was this a coincidence? Investigators didn't think so; they immediately felt it was a vital clue indicating that the killer was an artist from the Art Lover's Club. Reviewing the club's membership roll, they came across the name of 26-year-old Lucian Staniak, and when they searched his locker, they made a shocking discovery: a painting in red paint, just like that used on the letters, depicting a "disemboweled woman with flowers sprouting from her gaping belly".

Very reasonably concluding that they had their man, the cops caught up with Staniak on January 31, 1967, and hauled him off to jail. In police custody he openly admitted to his crimes, and even added to them, claiming to have killed as many as 20 people. This has never been proven, though, and in the event, Staniak was tried and convicted only for the deaths of the six known victims. On account of his deranged mental condition, he wasn't sent to prison but was instead confined to a mental hospital for the rest of his life.

The Feckless Crimes of Richard Speck

Born in Kirkwood, Illinois, Richard Speck began life in a happy home with his loving mother Mary and his attentive father Benjamin. But his world shifted dramatically when his father passed away when he was only six years old and his mother married a door-to-door insurance salesman named Carl August Rudolph Lindberg. Mary was quite smitten with Carl, but he was a man with a lot of baggage. Besides being an alcoholic, he had a long arrest record for forgery, drunk driving, and other offenses. Apparently blinded by love, Mary married him regardless and uprooted her kids to move to Carl's latest place of residence in Santo, Texas.

Over the next few years, the family bounced around at various locations within Texas. Besides the strain that constantly moving around put on Richard Speck, he was also frequently berated by his stepfather. His less-than-ideal home life soon affected his school life, and his grades deteriorated rapidly. His performance was so poor, in fact, that he ended up having to repeat the eighth grade. He did eventually make it to high school, but he dropped out in 1958, shortly after his 16th birthday.

By this point, Speck had become an alcoholic himself and was getting drunk just about every time he got the chance. He also followed his stepfather's criminal footsteps, quickly developing his own record for petty offenses—most of them related to alcohol. He did manage to hold down a job for a while, working at a 7-Up bottling plant for a few years. He also started a relationship with a young girl named Shirley Annette Malone, who soon ended up pregnant. Feeling that they had no other choice, the couple got married on January 19, 1962.

By this point, Speck's stepfather Carl had left the family and moved off to California. Speck's own child was born on July 5, 1962, but this new father wouldn't stick around his family for long either. In the summer of 1963, he was arrested for forging checks and given three years in jail. He ended up serving only half of his sentence before being paroled for good behavior in January of 1965. But once he got out, his behavior wasn't very good at all. Only a week after his release, on January 9th, Speck assaulted a woman with a knife. The woman got away and called the cops, and Speck was soon back behind bars. Found guilty of aggravated assault, he was given another 16-month sentence in addition to the parole violation. It was a comparatively light sentence for a violent crime, and due to sheer incompetence, it would get even lighter. Due to a clerical error that somehow only tabulated his time for the parole violation, Speck was released after just a few months.

Upon getting this second (or was it third?) chance, Speck initially seemed like he actually was trying to turn his life around. He got a job as a truck driver and was—at first—a decent, hardworking employee. That didn't last long, though, and soon he was messing up on the job. For one thing, he got into a string of (no doubt alcohol-fueled) accidents on the road; and on many occasions, he simply didn't come in to work in the first place. His marriage, meanwhile, had finally collapsed under all of the strain, and he moved in with a friend of his mother's.

On a definite downward spiral, Speck was soon arrested again for stabbing his opponent in a bar fight. The initial charge was once again aggravated assault, but his mother hired a skilled attorney who was able to get it reduced to disturbing the peace. That meant that Speck only had to pay a small fine and spend a few days in jail. That apparently wasn't enough to dissuade him from further crimes, and in March of 1966, he robbed a grocery store. Fearing that even his mother's slick lawyer wouldn't be able to get him off this time, he then left the state and headed up to stay with some of his relatives in Illinois.

His brother Howard got him a construction job, but rather than use the money to begin straightening out his life, Speck simply blew it on booze. When he was not working, he was a regular at the local dive bars. That spring he broke into the home of 65-year-old Mrs. Virgil Harris, held her at knife-point, tied her up, sexually assaulted her, and pocketed a whopping total of $2.50—apparently, all the old pensioner had in her possession. But as bad as Mrs. Harris's experience was, she was lucky to be alive, because Speck's next victim most certainly wouldn't be.

That was Mary Kay Pierce, a 32-year-old bartender who turned up dead on April 13, 1966. Mary Kay was a popular fixture at the neighborhood bar Frank's Place, and the regulars were all stunned at her demise. Well, except one. Speck was also a frequent patron of Frank's Place, and he (along with many others) was actually interviewed by police and asked what he knew about Mary Kay Pierce. Showing the signs of a true sociopath, this man who had so savagely killed Mary Kay was able to lie right to the faces of the police detectives. They were still able to find some inconsistencies in his story, however, and they began to consider him as a suspect in the murder.

Feeling the heat, Speck fled to Chicago, where he moved in with his sister Martha. Martha was married and had two young daughters, and she worked as a registered nurse in the children's wing of a local hospital. Speck kept his head down and stayed out of trouble for a while, but it didn't last. By the time summer rolled around, he was once again out drinking, carousing and getting into mischief.

On July 13th, he went totally off the rails. First, he pulled a knife on another patron of one of his hangouts, Ella Mae Hooper, forced her to come back to his room, and sexually assaulted her. He also stole her gun, which she'd never had a chance to draw. Leaving Ella Mae behind, he then broke into a nearby townhouse which served as a kind of dorm for student nurses. When the residents confronted him, he pulled his weapon and herded them all into a back room where he kept them for several hours. Then he systemically led them out one by one and murdered them. It's shocking that one man could so easily cow and kill eight people, but that's what happened. The only woman to survive was Corazon Amurao, who managed to hide under a bed.

Speck fled the scene, but he was quickly turned in by members of the community. At his trial in 1967, he was found guilty and given the death penalty. While he was sitting on death row, however, the state of Illinois decided to do away with capital punishment, and Speck's sentence was automatically commuted to life. Speck ended up dying of a heart attack on December 5, 1991, just before his 50th birthday.

Charles Schmid
The Pied Piper of Tucson

Charles Schmid was troubled from birth. Spurned by his biological parents, he was adopted by Charles and Katharine Schmid, but as it turned out he and his namesake didn't get along very well. In fact, it was partially due to this strain in the family dynamic that the Schmids divorced, leaving Katharine as the sole caregiver for young Charles Schmid. He felt bad about causing the family to break apart, and he developed feelings of guilt and inadequacy as a result.

These feelings grew considerably worse when a teenaged Schmid tracked down his biological mother—only to have her reject him. He had diligently done his homework to learn her identity and whereabouts, but a happy reunion was not in the cards. When Schmid showed up at his birth mother's door, she told him in no uncertain terms to leave and never come back. She made it quite clear to the traumatized young man that she did not feel responsible for him and did not want to be part of his life. One can only imagine how devastating this must have been, and it seems entirely possible that this was the moment that sent him over the edge.

Schmid's peers, on the other hand, generally liked him. He was a decent looking kid and a track star who wowed audiences with his speed. But in his senior year, he abruptly quit the track team, and just before graduating he was caught stealing stuff from the school's machine shop. He was suspended and never went back, and things deteriorated from there.

He seemed to have no direction in life, but he had plenty of money. His adoptive mother gave him an allowance of $300 a month—upwards of $2,500 in today's money. Since he was still living with her and didn't have to pay rent, he always had plenty of gas money for his motorcycle and drinking money for the bars that he frequented with his friends. His best buds at the time were his former classmates Paul Graf, John Saunders, and Richie Bruns.

While he wasn't in college, that doesn't mean he wasn't studying. It seems that Schmid spent most of his time learning how to manipulate others. He learned to be very charismatic and became a smooth talker known for chatting up the local young ladies. He also became obsessed with attempting to improve his appearance. He had always been self-conscious about his short stature, and now he took to wearing big cowboy boots filled with newspapers and flattened cans to increase his height. He also spent hours stretching his lower lip with a clothespin in an attempt to give himself a fetching lip curl reminiscent of Elvis Presley.

Eccentric though it may have been, all of this was harmless enough. But being a happy-go-lucky, all-expenses-paid bachelor cavorting with his friends wasn't cutting it for Charles Schmid. In the summer of 1964, he was looking for a new thrill in his life. Naturally, his mind went to murder.

Schmid was dating a girl named Mary French, who was friends with another girl named Aileen Rowe. Now he prevailed upon French to set Aileen up with his friend John Saunders. This, though, was just a ruse; Saunders was gay, and the only thing he and Schmid wanted to do with Aileen was to kill her. They brought her out into the desert on a double date, and then, while French waited in the car, Schmid invited Saunders to rape Aileen. Being gay, Saunders had no interest in doing that—but he wasn't averse to helping Schmid murder her. French then helped them both bury the body.

Aileen's disappearance resulted in a missing person case, never a top priority for law enforcement, and the investigation soon went cold. A few girlfriends later, however, when Schmid was dating one Gretchen Fritz, he confessed to her that he had murdered the missing girl. This led to a bit of blackmail on Gretchen's part later on; when Schmid attempted to leave her, she threatened to divulge everything that she knew about the case. Of course, blackmailing a murderer might not have been the brightest idea Gretchen ever had. Schmid promptly strangled her—and then strangled her sister Wendy for good measure.

Schmid apparently just couldn't keep his mouth shut, though. Soon he was telling his friend Richard Bruns all about his latest killings. Richard eventually ratted on Schmid, who was arrested, tried, convicted, and sentenced to death. In 1971, however, this sentence was commuted to 50 years imprisonment.

Schmid actually managed to escape from prison in the fall of 1972, when he and an accomplice briefly terrorized a family at their ranch in Tempe before being recaptured. Schmid's life came to an end a few years later after he was stabbed by a couple of other inmates on March 10, 1975. He died of his injuries several weeks later—a violent end for a man who had been consumed with a thirst for violence.

The Creepy Pasta of
Tony Costa

Tony Costa was a serial killer for whom some actually have a little sympathy. The case has been made that Costa's crimes were just a side effect of the 1960s drug-induced derangement. And Costa himself always maintained that he was not a killer by choice but had simply been caught up by forces beyond his control—a defense he continued to reiterate right up until he committed suicide in his jail cell. Is there any truth in any of this?

Tony Costa was born in 1944, during the height of the Second World War. His father was a soldier in that war, and as he died saving another man's life in combat, Costa never met him. As a child, though, Costa told his mother that a man would sometimes come to visit him at night, appearing at his bedside before suddenly vanishing. When his mother showed him a photo of his dead father, he cried out, "That's him! That's the man!"

Besides these alleged experiences with the paranormal, Costa had a fairly normal upbringing. His mother remarried, and she and her husband raised Costa in Cambridge, Massachusetts. As a teenager, though, he got mixed up with the wrong crowd, and by the time he was 16 he already had a criminal record for robbery and assault. But as

Costa came of age in the early 1960s, he cleaned up his act and found regular employment as a carpenter. He married in his 20s and went on to have three children. The marriage didn't last, but Costa's life remained fairly normal for a couple of years after the divorce.

Then several women in his community suddenly turned up dead. Costa would eventually be suspected of killing seven of them, although he was only found guilty of two murders, those of Patricia Walsh and Mary Anne Wysocki. Upon his arrest, Costa admitted that he was present when the two girls were killed but maintained that he wasn't the killer. He insisted that it was his friend "Carl" (who remains unidentified) who had killed them. According to Costa, the murders took place while he and Carl were hanging out with Patricia and Mary Anne and all four of them were "high on acid".

"Acid" is street slang for the hallucinogenic drug lysergic acid diethylamide, better known as LSD. This was the mind-bending drug of choice in the 1960s, advocated by everyone from philosophical guru Timothy Leary to psychedelic rockers such as the Beatles. But as much as pop culture was trumpeting the perception-expanding powers of LSD, the drug had a dark side. While many felt that their experiences on acid were revelatory and positive, others had what were called "bad trips".

Instead of feeling euphoria, the subject might experience terrible fear, paranoia, or extreme anger. The fact that they were locked into these feelings for several hours before the drug wore off only made things worse. People have described the feeling as if they had suddenly become insane—and many, unable to understand that this was just a temporary result of the drug they had taken, feared they had quite permanently lost their minds.

Costa contended that the mysterious Carl was having just such a bad trip when he completely flipped out and killed the two women. Costa said that he was eventually able to disarm Carl, but not before it was too late to save the girls. Patricia was already dead, and Mary Anne was writhing in her death throes. Costa asserted that it was out of a sense of compassion that he then picked up a knife to finish Mary Anne off and "end her suffering". Costa also claimed that another pair of women died from drug overdoses and then subsequently had their bodies mutilated and dismembered by that same crafty Carl. Costa stated that he wasn't present for this outrage, but his good buddy Carl told him all about it.

Aside from the fact that Carl couldn't be located, another problem with Costa's story was that the bodies were all found near Costa's own marijuana garden. Was all this just coincidence, circumstantial evidence that made an innocent man appear to be a deranged killer? That is admittedly hard to believe—and almost no one did believe it. After a quick trial in late 1969, Costa was found guilty of the murders of Mary Ann Wysocki and Patricia Walsh.

The deaths of the other women were never prosecuted, but authorities believed they had their man, and two murder convictions were enough to put him away for life. But this life in prison proved to be a fairly short one. Four years later, Tony Costa was found hanging from an improvised noose, dead by way of an apparent suicide.

Janie Lou Gibbs
The Cold-Blooded Killer

Born on Christmas Day, 1932, the joyful and always ready to please Janie Lou Gibbs was perceived as a true gift to her parents and their neighbors in her small town of Cordele, Georgia. No one ever imagined that she would ever grow up to hurt anyone—let alone become one of the most notorious serial killers of the 1960s.

Gibbs wasn't your average serial killer, though. She didn't kill with guns, knives, or ropes—she killed with poison. And she didn't kill strangers. From 1966 to 1967, she murdered her own husband, sons, and grandson. When her misdeeds were brought to light, the close-knit community of Cordele was horrified by her actions. Gibbs was a regular churchgoer who worked at a nursery school and also ran her own unofficial nursery out of her home. She was an unassuming and pleasing character, a stalwart pillar of her community. As one shocked neighbor said after her arrest, "She is a wonderful person. Very considerate, kind, congenial Christian as I knew her."

Gibbs began her life of crime by slipping some arsenic into her husband Marvin's meal at dinnertime. She was said to have been quite a

67

good cook, but little did anyone know what she was really cooking up! The ingredients she added to this particular dish weren't so much nutritious as they were deadly. Marvin became gravely ill and was taken to the hospital, where he at first appeared to be on the road to recovery. But after Gibbs brought him some homemade soup, his condition once again nosedived. Yes, you guessed it—that soup was full of arsenic. Marvin didn't stand a chance against this persistent poisoning program, and he was soon pronounced dead from liver disease.

Gibbs's church friends and others in the community felt sorry for the widow and showered her with attention and whatever aid they could render. Like any good sociopath, Gibbs relished the spotlight and lapped up all of the sympathies she could get. She also received a sizeable payout from Marvin's life insurance policy—part of which she donated to her church to thank them for all their support. As assiduously as she attended services, she must nonetheless have been absent the day her pastor covered "thou shalt not kill".

That wasn't the end of Gibbs's transgressions, either. Just a few months after her husband's death she started to poison her youngest son, Marvin Jr. The lad's health declined rapidly, and soon he was dead. Despite the back-to-back deaths in the Gibbs family, doctors did not become suspicious; they simply assumed that Marvin Jr. had inherited the same liver disease they believed had killed his father. In reality, of course, he had inherited the same twisted abuse from his murderous mother. But even when a third member of Gibbs's immediate family, her son Lester, passed away, no one suspected anything.

Gibbs was now down to just one son, Robert, who had recently gotten married and had a son of his own named Raymond. Robert and his wife were struggling to make ends meet, so when Gibbs offered to let them and their baby stay with her, they gladly accepted. This turned out to be a deadly mistake, but no one could have suspected the danger. Gibbs appeared to be a devoted and loving grandmother, and she certainly spent a lot of time with her new grandson. The only problem was that the little boy soon sickened and died. His father followed him in death by the end of the year.

Gibbs had been systematically putting small doses of arsenic into her grandson's baby formula and her son's morning coffee. Low doses of arsenic are not immediately fatal, but over time they accumulate in the body, making the victim seriously sick and eventually killing him.

It was only after the death of the previously healthy 19-year-old Robert Gibbs and his infant son that folks finally began to get suspicious of the woman they previously thought was simply unfortunate. After an official inquest, an autopsy was carried out on Robert which found that he had consumed arsenic. Considering the other deaths in her family, this was enough evidence to arrest Gibbs. She was taken into custody on her birthday, Christmas Day, 1967.

While Gibbs was passing the rest of the holiday season in a jail cell, her deceased family members were being dug up so that pathologists could have a second look. It was a grisly scene, with the exhumed corpses laid out on tarps and autopsied right there in the graveyard with the silent tombstones as witnesses. This fevered postmortem examination confirmed the worst: each of the deceased had a large amount of arsenic in his body.

Determined by a superior court jury to have significant mental impairment and deemed unfit to stand trial, Gibbs was whisked off to a psych ward. It was said that "she displayed no evidence at any time of feeling guilty about the alleged acts and could not understand herself as to why she did not feel guilty." In fact, the only thing she had to say on the matter was, "I don't question God's work. The Bible says they will get their reward, and I'm sure they will."

Apparently, in Gibbs's twisted mind, she had been doing God's work by killing five of her relations, as if God had somehow made her an angel of death! Most theologians (and just about anyone else in their right mind) would, of course, beg to differ. And interestingly enough, regarding the question of whether Gibbs was fit to stand trial, her old friends from church were some of the loudest voices insisting she was. They knew her best, and they insisted that she did indeed know right from wrong. Her own sister also pressed this point, and when visiting Gibbs in jail she would frequently try to get her to face up to what she had done, asking her directly, "Why did you kill your family, Janie?" But Gibbs refused to give her a straight answer.

Nevertheless, judgment in her case was temporarily deferred and she was placed in a mental hospital to receive treatment for severe psychosis. Here, this self-professed grim reaper passed her days rather peacefully. She was said to be a model patient who often helped out in the kitchen. As some have noted, it is rather remarkable that a woman who killed her family by putting poison in their food would be allowed to cook meals for other patients—but there was apparently no arsenic in the institutional pantry, and no further deaths were reported.

Gibbs lived at the mental facility for a number of years before she was eventually brought to trial.

Found guilty of five murders, she was given five separate life sentences, one for each life she had snuffed out. She remained in prison until 1999 when she was released on the grounds of her significant deterioration due to Parkinson's disease. Back on the outside, she lived with her sister until she was finally placed in a nursing home. Wheelchair bound and on oxygen, Janie Lou Gibbs, the woman who had shocked southern Georgia in the 1960s, passed away on February 7, 2010.

Give Peace and Love a Chance?

The 1960s were a time of great transition. The children of the World War Two generation, the Baby Boomers, had just come of age. When they themselves faced the prospect of fighting in the Vietnam War, they rose up to protest the establishment. Unlike their parents, who had dutifully served their nation with no questions asked, this generation was full of questions when it came to authority, the status quo, and the state of Western Civilization itself.

This was the era of "turn on, tune in, and drop out". The Boomers, the first generation that had grown up in front of the TV, seemed to believe that if you didn't like the current state of society all you really had to do was change the channel. But as much as the flower children would have liked nothing more than to bury their heads in their own psychedelic sands, there were real-life monsters lurking in the midst of all of their music festivals, freak-outs, and love-ins.

This book has followed the tracks that these killers made through the 1960s. No matter how much peace was being professed and sought, these psychopaths apparently didn't get the memo. Just like every other decade, the sixties had more than enough murder and mayhem in store. While the leaders of the counterculture wanted to give peace and love a chance, there were always plenty of wild-eyed miscreants ready to turn this hippie dream into a frightful nightmare.

Other books from Jack Smith from the Most Evil
Serial Killers by Decade series.

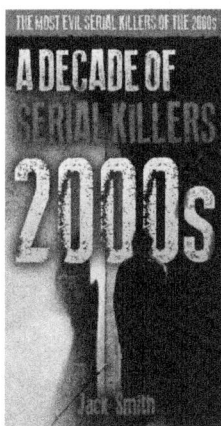

Printed in Dunstable, United Kingdom